adobe details

adobe details

karen witynski
joe p. carr

Gibbs Smith, Publisher

To my mother, Judith Simpson, and sisters,
Amy Witynski Holmes, Mara Witynski Schramm and Jenny Witynski. KW

To Joey Carr and Michael Carr. JC

First Edition

05 04 03 5 4 3 2

Published by
Gibbs Smith, Publisher
P.O. Box 667
Layton, UT 84041

Orders (1-800) 748-5439
www.gibbs-smith.com

Designed by CN Design

Printed and bound in Hong Kong

Library of Congress Cataloging-in-Publication Data

Witynski, Karen, 1960–
Adobe details / Karen Witynski and Joe P. Carr.—1st ed.
p. cm.
ISBN 1-58685-030-X
1. Adobe houses—Southwestern States. 2. Adobe houses—Mexico.
3. Interior decoration—Southwestern States. 4. Interior decoration—Mexico. I. Carr, Joe P., 1942– II. Title.
NA7224.6 .W579 2001
747.219—dc21

2001004582

Front Cover, top right: An ornately crafted tin mirror sparkles at the Westward Look Resort in Tucson, Arizona. Top left: A hand-painted Mexican headboard at Cíbolo Creek Ranch, west Texas. Bottom right: Old Native American pots rest in an artful built-in cupboard at Rancho Deluxe, Ribera, New Mexico. Bottom left: An adobe entrance arch is rich with texture and color at Misión del Sol, Cuernavaca, Mexico.

Front Flap: An old Huastecan water pot, Texture Antiques, Austin, Texas.

Back Jacket: An old Mexican bench and Navajo textile make a strong statement together at the Gage Hotel.

Half-Title & Title Page: The dining room at Rancho Deluxe features American Indian pottery and early American furniture.

contents

introduction

AFTER THE MEMORABLE EXPERIENCE OF LIVING WITHIN THE SENSUAL SURROUNDS OF A NEW MEXICO ADOBE HOME IN THE EARLY NINETIES, WE BEGAN AN EXPLORATION OF ADOBE DESIGN AND LIVING THAT HAS SPANNED MANY YEARS AND REGIONS, INCLUDING THE REMOTE MOUNTAINS OF MEXICO AND THE MESQUITE MESAS OF THE AMERICAN SOUTHWEST.

From Arizona ranches and rustic haciendas to colonial and contemporary homes, our adobe pilgrimage has revealed the popularity of adobe architecture and the rich design style that celebrates handcrafted details.

In recent years, pioneering architects, designers and builders have reinterpreted the world's oldest building material—adobe—in a seemingly endless variety of forms, thanks to its design versatility and eco-friendly potential. Although adobe can entertain a wide variety of interior design choices, the allure of the adobe home is grounded in grace and simplicity: softly contoured lines and thick walls shaped by hand, old-world architectural elements that come alive with hand-carved design details, and textural surfaces that become elegant backdrops for eclectic collections of antiques and colorful folk art. Outdoor "rooms" also express the elegant simplicity of adobe living: breezy *portales*, cobbled-stone courtyards and vine-covered *ramadas*.

Previous page, left: The warmth of adobe walls welcomes guests at the Hacienda San Francisco in Jalisco, Mexico. Right: Thick adobe walls create beautiful window openings. Designed by architect Gail Borst.

Opposite and right: A small built-in cabinet postures above a handcrafted bench by artist Nicholai Fechin. Fechin Institute and Museum, Taos, New Mexico.

alacena

Left: Palladian windows add a unique flair to this adobe home's covered portal. Designed by architect Ignacio Colin, Jalisco, Mexico.

Opposite: Hand-carved wood posts and adobe bricks create a natural statement on this elegant portal. Leggio residence designed by Steve Belardo, Rainbow Adobe.

ramada

Opposite and above: An outdoor dining room at Cíbolo Creek Ranch in west Texas is enhanced by a shady ramada.

Л. Б.

Opposite and left: The Ettinger adobe residence features exposed vigas that create dramatic striped light. Designed by Archaeo Architects.

Previous pages: A spacious sleeping porch at Cíbolo Creek Ranch in Shafter, Texas, features a collection of Mexican masks and antiques.

Designing interiors and furnishings for clients of our antiques gallery afforded us unique opportunities to explore firsthand the interiors of adobe luxury ranches, private homes, spa retreats, art studios, hotels and retail stores. We unearthed many modern adobes emerging from forward-thinking architects and builders and found a strong presence of traditional adobe interiors, including Spanish Pueblo and Territorial styles. From humble historical adobes to contemporary adobe "villas" and rammed-earth residences, adobe architecture embraces a variety of design details that celebrate the use of natural materials.

Our adobe experience continued through western Texas on excursions to the region's historical forts and old mining towns. Nestled amidst the Chinati Mountains, we discovered Cíbolo Creek Ranch, a historic adobe fort turned luxury resort, restored with authentic period details, Mexican and Spanish antiques, and an engaging collection of original artifacts and ranching implements that conjure a rugged romantic aesthetic. Nearby, we witnessed the adobe renaissance in the towns of Alpine, Marathon and Fort Davis, where old adobes have been rescued and revived as weekend homes.

Left: A small window creates interest in an adobe wall at Cíbolo Creek Ranch.

A tranquil courtyard is enhanced by a unique stone water feature. Holler and Saunders. Nogales, Arizona.

fuente

Left: Old Mexican doors add age and character to the Gage Hotel's Los Portales guest quarters.

Opposite: An old Mexican bench and Navajo textile make a strong statement together at the Gage Hotel.

At the Gage Hotel in nearby Marathon, a twenty-room adobe compound called Los Portales is designed around a Mexican-style courtyard boasting shady *portales* with intricately carved posts and incised corbels. Old Mexican doors add to the authentic air of a Mexican village with their rich character marks and round-headed *clavos* (hand-forged nails). Interiors feature traditional *viga* and *latilla* ceilings, Saltillo-tile floors, and colonial trunks and textiles.

Left: Tranquil open-air spaces are prevalent throughout the restored adobe forts at Cíbolo Creek Ranch.

Opposite: Hand-carved corbels and posts are design elements of the adobe home.

Misión del Sol, a serene Mexican spa resort, features adobe walls and architectural details.

While in Mexico photographing our second book, *The New Hacienda*, we crossed paths with many artful examples of innovative adobe homes both old and new, including two historic adobes in Oaxaca that have been beautifully revived by renowned artists. Although situated in diverse settings, these two restored adobes share a common thread as they celebrate natural materials with traditional, handcrafted details. In Cuernavaca, we were charmed by the design details at the Misión del Sol Resort and Spa. Throughout the eco-friendly retreat, the beauty of the exposed adobe brick and textural mud-plastered walls are subtle but definitive reminders of man's spiritual connection with the earth. Guest villas feature papaya-colored exterior walls and simple Mexican furnishings, including colonial trunks and once-utilitarian elements like tortilla and corn-grinding tables, as decorative accents.

GRANADA

UNION BOOK 1978
THE COMPLEAT McCLANE
TROUT
DICTIONARY

adobe design style

1

THE ESSENCE OF ADOBE STYLE IS A CELEBRATED USE OF NATURAL MATERIALS AND HAND-WROUGHT OBJECTS, AND A PARED-DOWN SIMPLICITY THAT EMBRACES AN ECLECTIC MIX OF CROSS-CULTURAL FURNISHINGS. ELEMENTS OF EARTH, STONE AND WOOD ARE THE INGREDIENTS THAT WEAVE TOGETHER TIME-HONORED DESIGN ELEMENTS WITH NEW-WORLD REFINEMENTS. SPECIAL RECIPES FOR EARTHEN FLOORS, NATURAL MUD AND LIME PLASTERS AND SURFACE TEXTURES ABOUND, LENDING TODAY'S ADOBE HOMES—BOTH RESTORATIONS AND NEW CONSTRUCTIONS—AN AIR OF OLD-WORLD CRAFTSMANSHIP.

Opposite: Warm melon-hued walls and a glowing fireplace beckon visitors to the inviting lobby at Santa Fe's Dos Casas Viejas.

Above: The flat surface of colonial Mexican baules or trunks offer unique display space for collections. Joshua Baer Gallery, Santa Fe.

From adobe walls hand-finished with sheepskins and polished with beeswax to hand-adzed *vigas* (ceiling beams) and furniture, the adobe dwelling has always been rich in textured surfaces and traditional markings that bear evidence of the human hand. Artifacts, pottery and decorative objects rest comfortably upon adobe's earthen walls and built-in *bancos* (benches) or inside *nichos* (niches) and *alacenas* (recessed cupboards).

Favored furnishings and accents are those that proudly reveal their character marks and patina. The key elements—tables, benches, *trasteros* (freestanding cupboards) and armoires—serve as stages for eclectic objects chosen with an eye towards authentic materials. From richly hued textiles and Pueblo Indian pottery to glazed ceramics, rustic ranching implements, and objects crafted from iron, copper or tin, decorative accents evoke a casual, timeless context. Native American beadwork and baskets mix with Hispanic traditions in religious woodcarvings to create a distinctive southwestern air. Favorite collectibles include *retablos* (two-dimensional paintings of saints), *ex-votos* (votive paintings commemorating miraculous events) and silver *milagros* (small charms representing devotional offerings), which are often encrusted on crosses of all sizes and, in some cases of artful expression, entire pieces of furniture.

Previous pages, left: A dramatically lit stairwell features ceramic tile steps in Malinalco, Mexico. Right: An eclectic collection of antiques and artifacts are showcased against a traditionally stepped adobe wall in a Santa Fe home.

Opposite: The Nogales, Arizona, residence of Holler and Saunders features an intriguing mix of antiques and accents, including a Peruvian chomba pot, a Mexican armoire and a Balinese carved deer.

Right: A Mexican bench holds court in an outdoor patio at the Gage Hotel in west Texas.

Glazed ceramics add rich, colorful textures to adobe interiors. These antique "tamalero" pots were formerly used for making tamales. Texture Antiques, Texas.

Milagros from Italy, Mexico, Peru, and New Mexico add dramatic interest to Gloria List's New Mexican trastero that dates from the early 1920s.

Adobe style melds together the best of past and present, deriving a great deal of charm from their contrasts. In their historic adobe in New Mexico's Mesilla Valley, Paul and Mary Taylor have skillfully mingled eighteenth- and nineteenth-century Mexican and New Mexican religious artifacts—*bultos* (carved representations of saints), *retablos* and crosses—along with artwork from present-day local artists. A deep appreciation for artistry both old and new is evidenced in the parlor and continues on through the music room, dining room and myriad hallways. A rich panoply of wood carvings, tin mirrors, Pueblo pottery, paintings and Navajo rugs surround early New Mexican furniture and old Mexican grain trunks.

milagros

Left: A santo from the eighteenth century postures inside a tin nicho on the fireplace mantel of the Taylors' adobe home.

Opposite: A simple wall pedestal holds an eighteenth-century santo in the Taylor residence.

santos

In artist Patrick Mehaffy and Erica Carol's restored 1890s adobe home, traditional details are enlivened with an eclectic collection of global art treasures. Earthen floors, hand-stenciled walls, and a partially exposed dining room wall reveal the authenticity of the home's original construction. Hohokam Indian stone paint palettes (stone devices used for grinding paint) rest in modern-shaped wall *nichos*, and an expressive mix of contemporary art blends easily with painted antiques, Aboriginal baskets, African masks, and Early American furniture, including a classic Shaker rocking chair. In the couple's dining room, a brightly painted wall cabinet features Peruvian animal fetishes at home with Zuni dough bowls. Throughout the home, down-to-earth elements such as a collection of heart-shaped stones add special touches to the artful surroundings.

Above: A collection of prehistoric stone axes and Hohokam paint palettes rest inside a framed nicho crafted from adobe plaster by Patrick Mehaffy.

Opposite: A decorative stencil and wainscoting brightens the kitchen fireplace of Rancho Deluxe.

repisa

In the Tucson home of Sue Adams, contemporary Guatemalan folk art postures atop an old Mexican *armario* (armoire) that charms with its worn layers of yellow paint. Across the Saltillo-tiled room, a hearty mesquite bench rests beneath a French painting, and a trio of hand-carved wise men rest on a wooden *repisa*, or wall shelf. Ceilings feature exposed *vigas* and saguaro ribs collected from the surrounding desert. The adobe walls are painted white and exude a special charm. The adobe blocks themselves are rounded, adding subtle contours to the surface. Intricately embossed tin mirrors provide a sparkling contrast to the textural walls.

Opposite: This antique Mexican bench anchors a bright corner of Sue Adams's living room.

Right: An old repisa, or hanging shelf, displays three wise men found in Sonora, Mexico.

a

Right: This hand-carved stone cross found in Mexico postures in Sue Adams's garden.

Opposite: A decorative iron grille lends beautiful contrast to the exposed adobe walls of the Adams home.

An avid gardener who entertains frequently, Adams embraces the "outdoor living room" as her favorite room of the house. Four sets of French doors lead to her treasured *portal* and private garden, complete with brightly upholstered furniture, a fireplace, and exotic cacti and tropical plants. Surrounded by an undulating adobe wall, the garden's peaceful center is a favorite stone cross that Adams discovered in a Mexican stone yard. Another serendipitous discovery, a wrought-iron grille from Chihuahua, Mexico, now decorates the garden entrance to Adams's master bedroom, serving as a secure and decorative trellis for the wildly growing fuchsia bougainvillea.

Opposite: Painted Mexican antiques add color and warmth to the Colemans' Tucson home.

Right: Design details of a Rio Grande blanket.

Antiques dealer and gallery owner Barry Coleman also finds the mix of past and present well suited for the adobe home he built for his family in the historic Fort Lowell district of Tucson. The contemporary red leather couch that anchors his artful living room contrasts with the rustic textures of Mexican furniture, religious artifacts, a hide-covered carriage trunk, and an antique cabinet filled with brightly colored trade blankets and Navajo rugs. Nearby, a lamp fashioned from an old East Indian corbel graces a brightly painted table, and textiles hang elegantly on a spotlit wall.

Opposite: A sequence of softly contoured adobe arches offer unrestricting views throughout the Leggio home, designed by Rainbow Adobe.

Right: Traditional Mexican glazed pottery adds elegant contrast to this modern adobe home in Malinalco, Mexico, designed by architect Hector Velazquez Graham.

ocotillo

Against the backdrop of adobe's simplicity, sensuous spaces easily integrate with nature. At Dos Casas Viejas in Santa Fe, a saguaro-cactus spine is suspended as sculptural art in the light-filled dining room, and closet doors feature intricate twig-branch shutters. In the Leggios' Texas home, a feathery tumbleweed crowns an old Spanish trunk in a shadowy play of textures. Also taking a cue from nature, Arizona architect Paul Weiner designed a contemporary fence for a Tucson client by joining sprouting ocotillo with simple iron bands for contemporary contrast.

Opposite: This sprouting fence of ocotillo creates a contemporary garden statement at a home in the Tucson mountains.

Right: A molasses mold is newly positioned as a planter in the stairwell of the Casa de la Torre in Cuernavaca, Mexico.

Left: A saguaro cactus skeleton found in the southwest desert adds natural elegance to the breezy dining room of Dos Casas Viejas.

Opposite: A raven head from the Tlingit tribe hangs as a sculptural element in the Ettinger home in Santa Fe.

textures

2

As the world's oldest building material, adobe has nurtured and sustained cultures throughout Mexico, Africa, South and Central America, the Middle East, and the American Southwest. Regardless of type—sun-dried adobe brick, rammed earth, cob, or compressed soil block—adobe's earthy textures provide homes with a timeless appeal.

Opposite: This reflecting pool sparkles as a brilliant kaleidoscope for the play of light and shadow upon exposed adobe walls. By Hector Velazquez Graham.

Above: A wrought-iron insect adds contrast to rammed-earth walls of a Tucson home.

Hand-carved by artist Nicolai Fechin, this door features a variety of design motifs. Fechin Institute and Museum, Taos, New Mexico.

Earth, stone and wood remain the building blocks of adobe homes today as they have been for centuries. These raw materials provide a palette of rich hues borrowed from the landscape and create depth and complexity inside adobe spaces, inviting a conscious and simple approach to interior design.

Opposite: Artist Patrick Mehaffy's leg sculpture adds artistic contrast to the texture of Rancho Deluxe's adobe floors.

Left: Decorative stencils add interest to a guest room's adobe fireplace at Hacienda San Francisco in Jalisco, Mexico.

The art of traditional mud and clay plasters, as well as mud floors, has been revived in recent years because designers and builders favor the rich textures and colors they bring new homes. Depending on the type of mud and clay used, the hues can range from white, beige, and yellow to red and even light green. Richard Connerty, of R. P. Connerty and Son Construction Company in New Mexico, frequently uses a micaceous clay to create custom wall surfaces that contain a subtle sparkle from the flicks of mica in the clay. Connerty has seen a strong resurgence of interest in traditional building methods and has created custom wall and floor surfaces throughout the country, including mud floors for Ralph Lauren's Polo Corporation home-furnishings showroom in New York City.

Textural variations in adobe surfaces also result from the use of a variety of plant fibers such as *paja*, or straw, as well as agave fibers, hemp, or cattails, which act as natural binders in adobe. Widely used for centuries to add strength and decoration to adobe walls, the technique of chinking—the placement of small stones or pottery shards in mortar joints—creates a natural lath for the application of mud or lime, and also produces beautiful surface patterns upon adobe, bringing richness and charm to even the humblest facades. Called *rajueleado* in Spanish, this technique is most commonly seen upon protective garden walls and in home exteriors.

Tucson's recently revived Barrio Santa Rosa features textural contrasts between adobe walls.

Small stones add rich texture and beautiful patterns to even the simplest adobe walls.

Adobe-walled streets in Mexico reveal the variety of wall artistry that can be created with simple stones and fragments at hand. In one section, small red, white and black pebbles are chinked into exposed adobe blocks in a repetitive sequence for dramatic impact. A contrasting example reveals slivers of red brick shards placed on the diagonal in accent to the adobe bricks. For a more formal look, a newly constructed wall also uses brick shards, but in this design uses a placement perpendicular to the earthen grid for graphic effect. Throughout the village and along the country roads, the various color and pattern accents of adobe walls are derived not only from chinking techniques but also from well-placed plantings of bougainvillea and trumpet vines that drape languidly over walls.

eleado

A celebration of local natural materials, Las Huertas features large wooden beams in a modern adobe home by Hector Velazquez Graham in Malinalco, Mexico.

vigas

The earthen walls that surround adobe homes have a subtle and profound effect on our daily experiences. Their softness of line echoes nature, and they become beautiful canvases for natural light. On outdoor terraces or patios, the sun creates geometric art through striped shadows issuing from rows of protruding *vigas*. Even shadows of large yuccas or aloe plants lend drama to exterior adobe walls and outdoor pathways.

Left: A brass bell tops an inviting entrance gate to the Meyerhoffs' Tucson, Arizona, home.

Opposite: An adobe outdoor stairwell features Saltillo-tile steps at the Meyerhoff residence.

The adobe home's casual outdoor spaces are prime for artistic expression and entertaining. Adobe walls beckon visitors to enter through spindled gates, often topped with bells and draped with a canopy of vines and plantings. Patios, courtyards and terraces feature ample entrances to promote the seamless transition from indoors to outdoors. The use of the same flooring materials—Saltillo tile, stone or brick—both inside and out further promotes the flow of space. In contrast to earthen garden walls, the use of sandstone block walls can create impressive stairways that double as flower-bed enclosures.

A dynamic water feature in a stacked stone wall at the Ettinger home in Santa Fe is set against a backdrop of adobe walls.

agua

Water features are also popular in all styles of adobe architecture, ranging from rock-lined *acequias* that wind their way through enclosed courtyards to simple bamboo spouts that trickle water onto single large stones. Intricately carved stone fountains are still favored for traditional courtyards, while modern adobes often feature multiple reflecting pools built into corners for both indoor and outdoor viewing. Spanish pot racks and old stone feeding vessels are easily adapted to garden planters, as are long *bebederos*, or wooden troughs.

furniture & architectural details

3

THE HANDCRAFTED DETAILS ADDED TO DOORS, CABINETS AND FURNISHINGS ARE INSTRUMENTAL IN GIVING DEPTH AND VISUAL INTEREST TO INTERIORS, SOFTENING EDGES AND SUMMONING EMOTIONAL CONNECTIONS TO SIMPLE MATERIALS AND SIMPLER TIMES. OLD IRON DOOR PULLS ON ARMOIRES OR TABLE DRAWERS, OR STRAP HINGES AND LOCK PLATES ON TRUNKS, ALL WEAR WELL WITH AGE AND PROVIDE AN AIR OF ANTIQUITY IN ADOBE SURROUNDS.

Rich with texture, this guest room at the Gage Hotel features colonial antiques and accents. Designed by Walton & Walton, Albuquerque, New Mexico.

Opposite: A simple nicho *in a rammed-earth wall holds an antique Mexican ceramic pot. Haas residence, Austin, Texas.*

Left: A sculptural fireplace celebrates strong color and adobe's handmade contours. The Taos Inn, New Mexico.

nicho

Early adobe homes were sparsely furnished and designed with simple built-in seating and storage. *Bancos*, or benches, of adobe were created as extensions of walls and were covered with blankets or sheepskins for comfort. Today, *bancos* take many sculptural forms, wrapping around corner fireplaces and surrounding kitchen tables and outdoor patios. Recessed wall *nichos* are also traditional features. Once holding religious saints and devotional objects, contemporary adaptations include square and shell-shaped *nichos* with decorative borders, as well as those large enough to hold books. *Alacenas* (built-in cupboards) were also prominent in old adobe homes. They were recessed into walls to hold kitchen implements and were usually covered with wooden-spindled doors. Variations on the *alacena* continue today, with brightly painted styles being popular for displays of ceramics, baskets and Mexican folk art.

Left: An early New Mexican trastero anchors the artful living room of the Taylor home.

Opposite: An Italian rock crystal chandelier adds sparkle to the minimal dining room of Gloria List's Santa Fe adobe.

Ponderosa pine was the most widely used wood for crafting furniture in the New Mexico region, as it was the most bountiful. Early simple furnishings included low, portable stools called *taramitas*, and rustic benches and chairs with laced rawhide seats. Trunks, chairs, tables and benches all featured mortise-and-tenon construction, as iron nails and hinges were scarce and expensive. The most common possessions were *cajas* (chests) or *baules* (trunks), used to store household possessions such as clothing and textiles. Most early trunks were plain and featured dovetail construction. Larger chests and grain storage trunks were designed with divided interior compartments for supplies. Popular floral and geometric design motifs carved into doors and furniture included X patterns, pairs of floral rosettes, pomegranates, and scalloped borders. Carved splats and spindles were prevalent on *alacena* doors and *trasteros* for ventilation.

fogón

This traditional corner fireplace and built-in banco create an elegant atmosphere in the sitting room of the Ettinger home in New Mexico.

Traditionally the heart of the home for warmth and cooking, the arched-hood corner fireplace has been a common feature in adobe homes since the Spanish introduced the *fogón* (fireplace) when they arrived in the New World. The elliptical opening and shallow fire pit require that logs be placed on end for burning, and this is the most popular style today. Adaptations over the years have yielded styles with sculptured two-tier mantels, tiled hearths and *nichos* for decorative objects and handy firewood storage.

Right: The vigas and latillas form a herringbone pattern in the ceilings of the Gage Hotel's Los Portales guest rooms.

Opposite: This intricately carved column is a testament to the fine craftsmanship of artist Nicolai Fechin. Located in Taos, Fechin's former home is now The Fechin Museum and Institute.

Hand-peeled logs were the earliest roof timbers used in adobe homes. Usually spanning fifteen feet in length, these round logs dictated the width of early homes. Traditional *viga* ceiling designs included a decking of smaller *latillas*, or crosspieces, that were placed in between the *vigas*. Made from aspen, cottonwood or cedar, these smaller poles were laid in either straight rows or herringbone patterns to form intricate, textured ceilings.

latillas

Rough-hewn serrated lumber adds a rustic decorative touch, and a simple cross formed of found wood is spotlit on an adobe wall at Café San Estevan.

Adobe walls and doors are enlivened by architectural accents.

This shady portal of Cíbolo Creek Ranch is anchored by a row of square wooden posts.

Overleaf: Antique iron plant stands, painted furniture and accents line the colorful portal of Maurice Dixon's New Mexico home.

portal

Decoratively carved architectural elements first appeared in mission churches and early aristocratic homes. Wooden beams and supporting corbels were often incised with rosettes and geometric and floral patterns, and occasionally featured natural dyes to accentuate the recessed detail. Decorative carving continues in popularity today and can be seen in rope-carved *portal* posts, window lintels, doors and mantelpieces. Many adobe building-supply retailers, including Old Adobe Pueblo Company in Tucson, Arizona, specialize in hand-hewn beams with a traditional southwestern look. Hewing is done on-site at the yard, where each timber is carefully worked by hand with an adze and edges are carefully draw-knifed and sanded to a soft, "hand-chinked" beam look.

An essential element of the adobe home, the *portal*, or covered porch, often spans the full length of the house or sometimes fills the space between two wings of a home. The long shaded *portal* of Maurice Dixon's New Mexico home is a favorite area for entertaining, as it provides casual seating amidst an artful mix of old Mexican ceramics, antique iron garden stands, and a whitewashed wooden farm table, usually topped with fresh produce from the garden.

An antique hand-painted Mexican head-board is rich with character and age.

C.

The weathered surfaces of old doors create a timeworn beauty in adobe rooms and add a compelling sense of history. After decades, or even centuries, of use, weathered, raised-panel surfaces and peeling layers of paint can reveal several underlying colors or hint at the color of the old wood. Hand-forged door handles and latches also offer a touch of old-world proportion and can be found today in a wide variety of styles.

In a world dominated by environmental concerns and fast-paced lifestyles, adobe's modern-day renaissance has been embraced for its sustainability and casual, sensual interiors that celebrate the warmth of natural materials and hand-wrought details.

resources

Our gallery and interior design firm, Texture Antiques, specializes in Mexican antique furniture, architectural elements and decorative accents. We offer extensive sources for old hacienda doors and gates, ceiling beams and hundred-year-old wood flooring. Additionally, harvest tables are made in custom sizes from reclaimed hardwoods.

www.casa-adobe.com

We invite you to visit our Web sites for design news, book previews and behind-the-scenes travel tips to Mexico destinations. In addition to previews of *Casa Adobe*, *Mexican Country Style* and *The New Hacienda*, our Web sites highlight adobe ranch hotels, adobe spas and Mexican hacienda hotels. We welcome your comments and questions.

Authors/Mailing Address
JOE P. CARR &
KAREN WITYNSKI
PO Box 162225
Austin, TX 78716-2225
(512) 370-9663
(512) 328-2966 fax

www.casa-adobe.com

Authors/Gallery and Design Studio
TEXTURE ANTIQUES
At Barton Springs Nursery
3601 Bee Caves Road
Austin, TX 78746
(512) 327-8284
(512) 328-2966 fax

www.mexicanstyle.com

Authors/Mexican Design Center and Colonial Retreat
HACIENDA PETAC
Yucatán, MEXICO
(512) 370-9663 (in Austin, TX)
(512) 328-2966 fax

www.hacienda-style.com

ADOBE RESORTS & HOTELS

CAFE SAN ESTEVAN
428 Agua Fria
Santa Fe, NM 87501
(505) 995-1996

CÍBOLO CREEK RANCH
P.O. BOX 44
Shafter, TX 79850
(915) 229-3737
www.cibolocreekranch.com

DOS CASAS VIEJAS
610 Agua Fria Street
Santa Fe, NM 87501
(505) 983-1636
www.doscasasviejas.com

THE GAGE HOTEL
101 Highway 90 West
Marathon, TX 79842
(800) 884-GAGE
(915) 386-4205
www.gagehotel.com

HACIENDA RANCHO DE CHIMAYO
PO Box 11, Country Road 98
Chimayo, NM 87522
(505) 351-2222

MISIÓN DEL SOL RESORT & SPA
Av. Gral. Diego Diaz Gonzalez 31
Col. Parres
Cuernavaca, Morelos,
62550 MEXICO
(800) 999-9100
www.misiondelsol.com.mx

THE TAOS INN
125 Paseo del Pueblo Norte
Taos, NM 87571
(800) TAOSINN
www.taosinn.com

WESTWARD LOOK RESORT
245 East Ina Road
Tucson, AZ 85704
(800) 722-2500
www.westwardlook.com

Previous page: Colonial glazed pots adorn a Mexican ranch table at Texture Antiques, Austin, Texas.

Above: Old beams from a colonial Yucatán hacienda have been finely crafted into a Spanish-style table by Joe P. Carr at Texture Antiques, Austin, Texas.

ORGANIZATIONS & RESOURCES

CALIFORNIA INSTITUTE OF EARTH ART AND ARCHITECTURE
10376 Shangri-La Avenue
Hesperia, CA 92345
(760) 244-0614
www.calearth.org

THE COB COTTAGE CO WORKSHOPS
Box 123
Cottage Grove, OR 97424
(541) 942-2005
www.deatech.com

CORNERSTONES COMMUNITY PARTNERSHIPS
227 Otero Street
Santa Fe, NM 87501
(505) 982-9521
www.cstones.org

EARTH BUILDING
5928 Guadalupe Trail NW
Albuquerque, NM 87107
(505) 345-2613
www.earthbuilding.com

EL RANCHO DE LAS GOLONDRINAS
334 Los Pinos Road
Santa Fe, NM 87505
(505) 471-2261
www.golondrinas.com

THE FECHIN INSTITUTE & MUSEUM
227 Paseo del Norte
Taos, NM 87571
(505) 758-1710
www.fechin.com

INTER-AMERICAS ADOBE BUILDER MAGAZINE & SOUTHWEST SOLAR ADOBE SCHOOL
PO Box 153
Bosque, NM 87006
(505) 861-1255
www.adobebuilder.com

NATURAL HOME MAGAZINE
201 East 4th Street
Loveland, CO 80537
(970) 669-7672
www.naturalhomemagazine.com

SUGGESTED READING

Contreras, Francisco Uviña, and Cornerstones Community Partnerships
Adobe Architecture Conservation-Handbook, 1998.

Easton, David
The Rammed Earth House
Real Goods/Chelsea Green Publishing, 1996.

Fathay, Hassan
Architecture for the Poor
University of Chicago, 1986.

Fechin, Eya
Fechin, The Builder
Fechin Art Reproductions, 1982.
Available through
Fechin Art Reproductions
PO Box 220
San Cristobal, NM 87564

Khalili, Nader
Ceramic Houses and Earth Architecture: How to Build Your Own
Cal-Earth Press, 1986.

McHenry, Paul G.
Adobe: Build It Yourself
University of Arizona Press, 1985. /
Adobe and Rammed Earth Buildings: Design and Construction
University of Arizona Press, 1989.

Seth, Sandra and Laurel
Adobe! Homes and Interiors of Taos, Santa Fe and the Southwest
Architectural Book Publishing Co., Inc., 1988.

Tibbets, Joseph M.
The Earthbuilder's Encyclopedia
Southwest Solaradobe School, 1989.

Weber, David J.
On the Edge of Empire: The Taos Hacienda of Los Martinez
Museum of New Mexico Press, 1996.

Witynski, Karen, and Joe P. Carr
Casa Adobe
Gibbs Smith, Publisher, 2001.

Witynski, Karen, and Joe P. Carr
Mexican Country Style
Gibbs Smith, Publisher, 1997.

Witynski, Karen, and Joe P. Carr
The New Hacienda
Gibbs Smith, Publisher, 1999.

Colophon: The body text was set in Gills Sans, designed by Eric Gill circa 1928. The chapter titles were set in Matrix Bold, designed by Zuzana Licko circa 1986, and the captions were set in Matrix Script.

Overleaf: Hand-carved Virgin of Guadalupe by Alfredo Rodriguez. Collection of Ann Bahan, Austin, Texas. Photographed at Barton Springs Nursery.